Contents

The Third Week of Advent

The Fourth Week of Advent

[Readings are identified by Week and Day of Advent, rather than by date, to allow this book to be used again in any year. In such instances, however, adjustment will need to be made for fewer, or more, days in the Fourth Week. Advent begins four Sundays before Christmas Day.]

Greetings from the Principal

Advent greetings from the Nazarene Theological College. I am writing this in a large shopping centre in Manchester where a sign nearby asks, 'Is your home ready for Christmas?' It is early October.

The retailers are already hard at work planting thoughts of preparation in the minds of the shoppers and playing on emotive themes of the season. Many people however, approach this time with a mixture of anticipation and dread. Preparation costs money and there is the usual rush to get things ready on time. Being 'ready' may elude many of us!

We send you this gift of Advent readings in the hope that these may help you focus on the giving of the greatest gift of all, the Lord Jesus Christ. In preparing for Christmas, may you find time for self preparation as you reflect not only on Christ's advent but also the promise of his coming again.

Each writer and all of the college family joins together in thanking you most warmly for your prayers and support through this past year. May this Advent and Christmas season be one of rediscovery of the meaning of Christmas.

'When the time had fully come, God sent His Son' – Galatians 4:4.

David McCulloch,
Principal

Introduction

With this book of meditations, we invite you to join together with us, and the Church universal, in Advent worship. The word 'Advent' derives from the Latin *adventus*, which means 'coming'. The season proclaims the comings of Christ – his birth which we prepare to celebrate again, his coming continually in the Word and Spirit, and his return in final victory. Therefore, Advent looks both backward to Jesus' first coming at Bethlehem and forward to His coming again at the end.

The readings given here are those of the common lectionary for each day, so we are literally reading from the same page with millions. You will find that the readings for Advent deal not so much with preparation for Christmas as with the expectation of Christ's return in glory to rule, judge, and save. There is a strong prophetic note in this season announcing judgement upon evil, combined with an emphasis on hope and the expectation of Christ's coming reign in glory.

NTC Faculty and Staff and NTC alumni from around the globe have contributed to this booklet of devotion. As you read, and pray, we hope you will include NTC in your prayer this month, as every month, as we seek to tell out the good news of Jesus Christ until he comes.

Dwight Swanson, Editor

Darkness and Christmas

Amos 1:1-5, 13-2:8; 1 Thess 5:1-11; Luke 21:5-19

This first day of readings paints a stark picture of our world. It isn't exactly the picture we want to think about as we approach Christmas. We tend to gravitate toward warm feelings and cosy comforts, traditions and family and good memories. It's the one time of year when we can be unabashedly sentimental.

On the other hand, it is perfectly appropriate in the Advent season to consider the actual reasons for Jesus' coming into the world, and in response, to hope and pray for his soon return. After all, Jesus didn't descend from on high merely to give us a warm-fuzzy holiday. He came to save us from ourselves, from the destruction and chaos we inflict on one another. In fact, to save us from the world described in today's passages.

Unfortunately, that world is not lost in the mists of ancient history. As you're reading this, it is likely that, just as in Amos, a pregnant woman somewhere in the world is being attacked and ripped open; someone living in desperate poverty is being sold into slavery; a girl is being raped by both a man and his son. We are aware of great earthquakes, famines and plagues, as Luke describes, and of believers being arrested and persecuted. We shouldn't have to work too hard to relate to this picture of our world.

And still, in our passage from 1 Thessalonians, Paul acknowledges that we believers sometimes succumb to the temptation to be insulated from all of this horror. He challenges us, saying, 'But you are not in darkness, for that day to surprise you like a thief'. In other words, don't be lulled into believing this is just the way of the world, and so become desensitised to it. Rather, acknowledge the horror, and welcome Jesus into it. His arrival — both the first one, and the second still to come — is about ripping away the veil between heaven and earth, so the burning, purifying light of God's love and peace can pour into our dark world. Come, Lord Jesus!

Sarah Derck,
Chaplain

'When a poor man came in sight...'

Amos 2:6-16; 2 Peter 1:1-11; Matthew 21:1-11

A preoccupation with getting people 'born again' can result in neglecting the great body of biblical teaching on social justice and concern for the poor and the stranger within the gates. Christmas is 'peace on earth, goodwill to all people'. The good news is for all! And the teaching of Scripture on inclusion and human rights is accompanied by God's abhorrence of, and judgement on, a people who are selfish, corrupt, and uncaring.

Sadly, the state of affairs, vividly described by Amos, parallels the state of our nations today. Our politicians have bent and abused the rules, greed and the self-centred mind-set can be found at every level of society, and the needs of others are forgotten. The sin and selfishness of the people are all the more tragic in the light of the goodness of God – 'I brought you up out of Egypt, I led you... I gave you' (Amos 2:11).

However, it is possible to live the life that is pleasing to God and to be sensitive to the needs of others – and not only at Christmas time. 'His divine power has given us everything we need for life and godliness' (2 Peter 1:3). The gospel imperative of loving our neighbour is possible. To demonstrate concern for the poor and marginalised is the outworking of grace on our journey. The process of spiritual addition mentioned by Peter includes brotherly kindness and love (2 Peter 1:7).

The journey that Jesus took, from heaven to Bethlehem to Calvary, is an example to us that surrender and sacrifice is God's way and His will. The so-called 'triumphal' entry in Matthew 21 was not only a fulfilment of prophecy, but an act of obedience and humility. The paradox of 'meekness and majesty' – the king and a donkey – leads through passion week to a cross of shame. And this is our God the 'servant' king.

Service and suffering are characteristics of the Christ-like life. We need to be concerned for the whole person and for the needs of others. Good King Wenceslas had it right.

Colin Wood,
District Superintendent, British Isles North,
Chairman of the Board of Governors, NTC

Listening again to familiar words

Amos 3:1-11; 2 Peter 1:12-21; Matthew 21:12-22

It amazes me that I can remember the words to Christmas carols despite only singing them once or twice a year. Yet I fail to remember things I repeat more frequently, such as the names of people I meet weekly, or how to spell particular words. These hymns tell a story, familiar to me and to other Christians, of Christ's birth and of the promise that there will be a time when he will return again in glory. I can't identify how these hymns have imprinted their words and tunes into my memory but I am left with a feeling that their familiarity leads to a blasé understanding of their message; only occasionally do I remember to pause and consider what I'm singing or question the meaning of particular phrases.

There is a challenge from Peter to refresh our memories and remember the power, importance and relevance of Christ in our lives, no matter how mature our faith or how familiar we may think we are with the truths to which Peter refers. As we enter this Advent season, what better time to consider the beginning of our personal experiences, understanding and knowledge of Christ in our lives.

However, this should be based on more than an individual interpretation or our own nostalgic thoughts. Our remembering should also involve listening to the voices of the prophets, the voices of those who were eye-witnesses to the person and the majesty of Jesus, and not least by looking afresh at the written records of Jesus' authority in action. Together these voices and examples serve to remind us not only of the past and the foundations of our faith but of the crucified and risen Christ at work in our world today; the revelation of God's plans in this 21st Century.

Spend some time in silence, and then think of some of the ways in which your faith is confirmed, perhaps through scripture, science, reason, history, and personal testimony. Consider your relationship with God at this time, how do you hear the voice of God and, crucially, how do you respond?

Louise Kenyon,
Lecturer in Youth Ministry,
Youth Ministry Course Coordinator

More secure than the Bank of England

Amos 3:12 – 4:5; 2 Peter 3:1-10; Matthew 21:1-11

A contradiction exists in business finance. On one hand, when forecasting for the year ahead, we spend considerable time attempting to predict the unpredictable. In this, mere promises are discounted, for we try to eliminate risk and focus only upon facts. On the other hand, the world of finance exists upon promises. You only have to look at a £5 note, which is merely a promissory note bearing the words, 'I promise to pay the bearer on demand the sum of five pounds'. Can these two seemingly incompatible views be reconciled?

The answer of course is yes, for if it wasn't so, our financial worlds would collapse. The promise on a £5 note is supported by a signature that has value, that of the Chief Cashier of the Bank of England. Centuries of history, during which the promise has been honoured time and time again, give this signature the value it generates and full confidence in this promise.

In 2 Peter 3:4, Peter writes of those who question a promise of Jesus to come again, not as a baby in a manger but in his full glory as the King of Kings and the Lord of Lords, before whom every knee shall bow.

The question, 'Where is this "coming" he promised?', is still on the lips of people today. To answer this we must also refer them to the evidence of history, just as we do with a £5 note, and demonstrate the value of the 'signature' on the promises of God, all of which have been fulfilled.

During Advent, we celebrate the birth of Jesus, and rightly so, but can we place our trust in his promise to return again? He will come like a thief in the night, when we least expect it. Are we ready? Is it a promise we can put our faith in? Next time you spend a £5 note, look at the promise it contains, but remember this more, the last recorded words of Jesus are another promise, 'I am coming soon!' Are we ready?

I Barrie Thomas,
Financial Manager, NTC,
Director, The Living Well Trust, Carlisle

Hastening the Day

Amos 4:6-13; 2 Peter 3:11-18; Matthew 21:33-46

The theme of God coming in judgement runs through today's readings. In Advent, the Church prepares to celebrate the First Advent, the coming of the Lord as a babe in a manger in Bethlehem, but it looks forward to the Second Advent, the coming again of the Lord as Judge in power and might. We are to examine our discipleship in the light of that coming day.

2 Peter describes 'the coming day of God' in disturbing images – the heavens being set ablaze and the elements melting with fire – which emphasise the awesome lordship of the God who has come to us in Jesus Christ. This should lead us to pray for God's mercy not only for all that displeases him in our personal lives but also for his mercy on all who displease him in society around us. Yet, judgement is not God's final word. 2 Peter leaves us with a vision of the future God intends for us: 'We wait for new heavens and a new earth, where righteousness is at home'.

Our readings show us the character of this new creation – righteousness, peace, justice, holiness and truth – and is continuous with what we already know of God from the OT prophets, e.g., Amos; and above all from the earthly life of Jesus – the one through whom this will be ultimately fulfilled.

2 Peter challenges us actively to shape our lives on this vision, because (staggeringly!) by so doing, we in some way actually 'hasten the coming of the day of God'! That is, we are to live out that future here and now – holiness of life and being a committed follower of Christ matters for, in some mysterious way, it hastens the Second Advent. May the conviction of the author of 2 Peter be our conviction – that the day of God will come and in the end Christ will be all in all.

In this season of Advent, let us work and persevere in our discipleship 'until (that) day dawns and the morning star rises in (our) hearts' (2 Peter 1:19).

Don Maciver,
Librarian

Seek God and find life

Amos 5:1-17; Jude 1-16; Matthew 22:1-14

Amos proclaims, 'Seek me'(v 4). Who is this me? Amos goes on in v 6 to tell us that it is the Lord. Later on he says that we are to seek good. All three references indicate that seeking the good Lord results in life. 'Seek me and live; seek the Lord and live; seek good, not evil, that you may live.'

When we take steps towards seeking God we will discover that it is not difficult to find him. He is not hiding from us. In fact, Jesus, in his parable of the wedding feast (Mt 22), implies that God has issued an invitation for us to be part of the Kingdom. In his parable, Jesus has the king, surely representing God the Father, sending his servants to those who had been invited to the banquet to tell them to come.

Why have we been invited by the good Lord? Jude uses the word 'called' and says we have been called because we are loved by God the Father and the promise is that we will be kept by Jesus Christ (v 1).

The tragedy of this, and every, Advent season is that many will hear about Jesus but not really seek him; many will accept all kinds of invitations except the most important one – they will refuse to come into the kingdom of the God who loves them.

Jude records that Enoch warns us, 'See, the Lord is coming with thousands upon thousands of his holy ones to judge everyone, and to convict all the ungodly of all the ungodly acts they have done in the ungodly way, and of all the harsh words ungodly sinners have spoken against him.'

In this Advent season, a season of spiritual preparation, the message of Amos is to seek God and find life; the message of Jesus is 'You have been invited'; and the message of Jude is 'You have been called and Jesus will keep you'. Don't miss out.

Geoff Austin,
Pastor, Ardrossan,
British Isles North District

Waiting for a better day

Amos 5:18-27; Jude 17-25; Matthew 22:15-22

The short letter of Jude is best known for its closing verses, a benediction often delivered in solemn tones by the minister at the close of a worship service. Sometimes forgotten are the preceding verses, a call for Christians to persevere through tough times. Part of perseverance is patiently waiting for a better day: 'Keep yourselves in God's love as you wait for the mercy of our Lord Jesus Christ to bring you to eternal life' (Jude 21). While this world may bring unjust suffering for the righteous, the next will balance the scales, a new creation where Christ will re-order all things.

Amos 5 forecasts a darker outcome for some. The court system in Israel was a sham. The poor were denied justice since the guilty paid a bribe (v 12). Further, the people thought they could worship multiple gods, offering sacrifices to the Lord and to idols (vv 25-26). This gave them false confidence, an anticipation of the Day of the Lord as a time of light, yet Amos forecasts darkness. They would be like a man running from a lion, only to meet a bear (v 19). Divine justice would arrive like a mighty river.

While the present age makes comfort the ill-gotten fruit of injustice, the future age promises a new value system. The afflicted will be comforted and the comfortable afflicted – see Luke 15:25. Yet how are we to live between the incarnation and the Second Coming? By paying taxes (Mt 22:15-22), Jesus respected civil authority, yet maintained a loyalty to his Father, the final Authority. He spoke of yeast that works its way through the whole batch of dough (Mt 13:33), as well as salt and light (Mt 5:13-16). These images call us to influence those around us peacefully, modelling righteousness in a world that too often is unjust. Like Jude and Amos, we invite others to live, remembering that our loving and just God will reconcile all accounts. During Advent, we focus on the One for whom we wait. Christ has come; Christ will come again. What a hope!

Greg Crofford,
Director, Nazarene Theological Institute,
French Equatorial Africa

Wondering whether God will really act

Amos 6:1-14; 2 Thess 1:5-12; Luke 1:57-68

December 1st and Christmas already seems to be here! Advent gets squeezed. But for Christians, it is important. Advent addresses some challenging themes.

Amos lived during economy prosperity. Powerful people enjoyed the good times. After all, prosperity was a sign of God's good pleasure – they were a blessed nation. So, Amos' words shocked: Alas for those who are at ease in Zion, and for those who feel secure on Mount Samaria. Beneath the veneer was a system maintained by violence and oppression. Leaders ignored the poor while living lives of conspicuous consumption. But God commanded Israel to care for the marginalised. His demands were few but far-reaching: act justly, love mercy and walk humbly with God. However, says Amos, you have turned justice into poison and the fruit of righteousness into wormwood. In our cities beneath the glitter of Christmas shopping – our own being at ease in Zion – exists an underclass of people: asylum-seekers, addicts, ex-offenders, homeless. What might Amos say to us this Christmas?

For his part, Paul writes directly to the underclass, people suffering for the gospel. Paul thinks this is normal. Christians suffer because they announce the gospel in the face of organised rebellion against God. Paul does not pray that they will escape suffering. Neither does he promise revenge. Rather, Paul prays that God will make them worthy of his call as agents of the gospel, that they will be filled by God's power so that they can stand firm, all to the glory of God. This is good news. Suffering is not the end for Christians. God's good purposes will triumph.

And so, aging Zechariah, filled with the Holy Spirit, announced that John's birth was the sign that God's good purposes were about to be set in motion. God is at work – not only through John. He has acted decisively in Jesus.

What a special child! And what faithful people, even in the face of decades of discouragement and wondering whether God was really at work. We are called to follow Jesus in holiness and righteousness. Will we too be faithful?

Kent E Brower,
Vice-Principal,
Senior Lecturer in Biblical Studies

Living in constant expectation

Amos 7:1-9; Revelation 1:1-8; Matthew 22:23-33

The people of God live in constant expectation. Christians are expecting people. They are people of hope. There is always a sense in the Christian faith that something is about to happen. A sense in which a new era is about to break in and the break-in is imminent. There is also a sense in which the expected new era is better than the present era. It will be a reversal of present chaos and disorder.

Sometimes we look at the world around us and see news headlines, reports on poverty, sickness, violence, abuse, tribulation, oppression, depression, war, etc., and wonder where the world is leading and whether God is still in control. John's doxology reminds us the most important thing: The triune God is the one 'who is, who was, and who is to come' (vv 4, 8).

1) The Lord is: In the midst of the disorder and strife in the world the Lord is alive. He is the great I AM. He is real here and now in our present circumstances. He is the one who has loosed us from sin and raised us to be a kingdom of priests. He is the first and the last.

2) The Lord WAS: He is the ancient of days. He has seen and known what we have not. He has been through the best and worst. He is the witness on whom we can rely because he speaks from first hand knowledge. He was dead and is now alive. He rose again in an imperishable body never to die again. He is the firstborn from the dead. He sits at the right hand of the Father.

3) The Lord IS TO COME: He is to come again and his second coming will be victorious. All his enemies will lament in remorse while those who waited patiently for him will rejoice. The people of God are to walk in confidence as they wait in anticipation of the Lord's second coming.

Musa Kunene,
Research Student,
Swaziland

Pray for the persecuted

Amos 7:10-17; Revelation 1:9-16; Matthew 22:34-46

The Church of Jesus Christ awaiting his Second Coming is a persecuted church. It is estimated that in the past year 176,000 Christians were martyred for their faith.* Persecution is the theme which links together today's readings.

Amos' integrity is challenged by Amaziah the priest of Bethel. Amos' famous response (vv 14-15) places the emphasis on his calling from God. Christians facing persecution today find strength in their calling from God to testify to the truth of the Gospel.

Jesus also faced challenges to his personal integrity (v 16). Today's reading, continuing the testing questions of the Pharisees, elicits from Jesus the brilliant and original response which combines a holistic love to God and neighbour. Jesus then responds by showing that the Pharisees are not clear about the identity of the Messiah they are defending. Christians today must respond to the unjust accusations of their persecutors with the love of God for their enemy as neighbour (Mt 5:43-48).

The early Church was born into persecution. The message from the Lord of the Church (v 18) in the Book of Revelation, to the seven churches of Asia minor (v 11), through the prophetic ministry of John (vv 9-11), begins with a vision of the Risen Lord which stresses his power and authority. It is difficult to picture the vision described, but the elements should be seen as verbal rather than visual symbols (vv 13-16). This vision gives us confidence to pray for our persecuted brothers and sisters this Advent season.

*David B. Barrett, Todd M. Johnson & Peter F. Crossing, 'Christian World Communions: Five Overviews of Global Christianity, AD 1800 - 2025,' *IBMR* 33/1 (2009), 32.

Christopher Cope,
Learning Support Tutor,
Bookshop Manager

A famine for hearing

Amos 8:1-14; Revelation 1:17-2:7; Matthew 23:1-12

The Bible remains the No. 1 bestselling book of all time, with more than 6 billion copies sold. Yet according to an anonymous survey carried out in England in the 1990's among Evangelicals, 90% confessed to not opening their Bibles from one Sunday to the next. I'm not sure that a survey done in Scotland, N. Ireland, or the USA would have yielded better results.

Is there a famine for hearing the Word of the Lord? The dictionary says that a famine is a dearth or shortage – a need for something that's missing. Perhaps it's not so much a famine as spiritual anorexia. Anorexia is a loss of appetite, and surely Christians are losing their appetite for the Word of God. Anorexia is virtually unknown in the Majority World. Where there is a genuine hunger people feed on what is available to assuage their hunger. People with anorexia tend to live in a land of plenty. Here in the West we are surrounded by food of every variety in the supermarkets and in our homes, yet the anorexic refuses to eat it. They play around with it on their plate, and derive very little nourishment from it. As a result they become weak, losing not only muscle and stamina, but their zest for life. They feel cold all the time.

The same symptoms trouble the spiritual anorexic. They may have several Bibles lying around their homes, and may even have Bible reading notes or devotionals, but they do not feed on them. They lose spiritual stamina, muscle and their zest for life in the Lord. There is coldness in their hearts for the things of God.

In countries where Christians are persecuted the Word of God is held in such high esteem, that if only one Bible is available, they tear the pages out and share them so that every believer has their own supply of spiritual food.

Are you in danger of becoming a spiritual anorexic? What keeps you back from hearing and feeding on the Word of God? Is it laziness, or TV? Family or work commitments? Remember, 'Faith comes by hearing, and hearing by the Word of God'.

Maggie Vosper,
Pastor, Edinburgh,
British Isles North District

A word from the impatient about waiting

Amos 9:1-10; Revelation 2:8-17; Matthew 23:13-26

When I was a youngster, Advent seemed all about waiting: counting the days until Christmas, seeing doors on the Advent calendar opening one at a time. Some people are good at waiting. My mother was always incredibly patient. But I'm not the most patient of individuals. I'm often in a hurry…

When the coffeepot is slowly filling up on a Monday morning – drip, drip, drip – I can't wait until it gets to the top. I pull it out early, and get the really strong stuff. When someone is tootling along the road in their car at twenty-three miles an hour, admiring the view, I'm desperate to get past them, revving my engine. When the bank teller at Barclays decides to have a nice little chat with the elderly lady in front of me, I feel my blood pressure rising. And when things don't happen as quickly as I think they ought – in my home, my church, at College, then sometimes I get frustrated, impatient, irritated.

It's easy to become impatient for God to step in and set things straight. What's God up to?

In dark times, Advent helps renew our hope. We're waiting for God to act, to step into his world again, like that first Christmas.

Our Christian faith carries a promise: the waiting period we're living in won't last forever. Hang on, God says, I am coming soon. In the meantime, Jesus invites us to be prepared, to keep our focus on what really matters.

And we must watch. Christ is continually moving into our lives. On that final day, it will be obvious who he is. We'll slap our forehead and say 'of course!' as things fall into place like the last scene of an Agatha Christie novel. All will confess that Christ is Lord.

In the meantime – He appears to those who receive the gift of watching and waiting and use it to do just that – to watch, to wait, to read their lives from top to bottom in the light of his being there.

Peter S Rae,
Dean

Here's looking at you, Kid

Haggai 1:1-15; Revelation 2:18-29; Matthew 23:27-39

My Pastor comes from Wales. All of her family live there, while she works and ministers in Scotland. A couple of years ago her pastoral duties meant she would not be going home for Christmas. I heard her talk about the gifts she was planning to send. As I was going to the south Wales area to conduct a wedding service the weekend before Christmas I asked her if I could help by delivering the gifts on her behalf. So she arranged for her dad and me to meet in a retail car park on the outskirts of Cardiff.

As I had never met her dad, nor he me, the plan was that I would go to a free area of this car park and he would come and drive up beside my car. I was to watch for a red car arriving around 10 a.m. I arrived, and waited for the red car. A short time later a red car drove past many empty spaces to one just beside me, and stopped. Out stepped a tallish man dressed in black tight trousers (not what I'd expected), and I approached him with arms outstretched to say, 'Hello!' He, however, quickly said, 'I'm not who you think I am!!!' It got me thinking, 'Am I who you think I am?' Are we who people think we are? There is an old adage that says looks can be deceiving! Things are not always what they appear to be. This might be true in our lives. What we portray may not always be in line with who we are in reality, or perhaps more importantly what God is calling us to be.

In Revelation 2 the Spirit was concerned with the misleading appearance given to those looking on at the church by one in the god business who called herself a prophetess but misrepresented the truth by her teaching. In the Gospel of Matthew Jesus was concerned by the misleading appearance given to those looking on at religion by those in the god business who were not all what they said others should be. The prophet Haggai was concerned with those who were caught up with the appearance of their own place but not God's.

This Advent season may be an appropriate occasion to prepare for Christmas by taking a look at the person in the mirror and, as the prophet Haggai writes: 'Give careful thought to your ways'.

Tommy Goodwin,
Chaplain, Royal Navy

Wake up!

Haggai 2:1-19; Revelation 3:1-6; Matthew 24:1-14

I see most people anticipate and enjoy Christmas. To my surprise, people outside the church usually make more noise than the believers at Christmas. Often I wonder whose festival Christmas really is. People have fun at Christmas, having parties, sharing gifts and so on and so forth. But when it comes to the issue of the coming of the Christ and the final judgement, many people make fun of Christians. They seem to want to have fun, but have no interest at all in any of the serious issues of Christmas.

Here in Mt 24:3, Jesus' disciples are exceedingly serious about the end of the age. In response to their interest, Jesus warns his disciples not to be afraid when the signs occur. Having read this, questions come to my mind: Are the 21st-century disciples as serious as the disciples in the first century were about the end of the age? Or do we see the signs of the last days with fear in our hearts? I now see the signs that Jesus once told to the disciples: wars, famines, and earthquakes in various places. However, I do not seem to perceive the seriousness of the signs. Often preaching on the day of judgement with the second coming of the Christ, I admit that I am honestly not excited, but am somehow indifferent. Have I fallen into a slumber?

All of a sudden, I hear a call from the Lord, 'Wake up!' (Rev 3:2) and listen to his voice: 'The end will come when the gospel of the kingdom will be preached in the whole world as a testimony to all nations' (Mt 24:14). However, watch out! 'You will be handed over to be persecuted and put to death, and you will be hated by all nations because of me' (Mt 24:9), says Jesus. What a paradox! Jesus says that the final victory comes when the signs do not appear to be so victorious. We, Christian churches, have a reputation of being alive but we are dead unless we prove to be alive, showing our deeds complete in the sight of God, by remembering what we have received and heard and faithfully obeying it (Rev 3:3a).

Wake up! As Jesus said to his disciples, the Spirit says to us today, 'Whoever has an ear, let them hear what the Spirit says to the churches' (Rev. 3:6).

Oh Won Keun,
Pastor, Pyoung Taek, Korea

Living between the times

Amos 9:11-15; 2 Thess 2:1-3, 13-17; John 5:30-47

Which of the following is most likely the 'Man of lawlessness'? a) Mahmoud Ahmadinejad; b) Nicolae Carpathia; c) Barack Obama. If only we could be sure! Or, at least it seems that many think it would be helpful to be able to fit names to clues of Jesus' Coming. But, then, the names have changed so many times just in the past forty years that one is left doubting that it matters.

Amos and Paul leave clues that matter. But, they are contrasting clues, and lead to something even more important than names. Firstly, the Amos reading, written before the destruction of judgement fell on Israel, portrays the Day of the Lord as bringing a day of joy and blessing after judgement (it appears that even Nazarenes will drink the plentiful wine of that day!). Then, Paul presents the Coming of our Lord Jesus as a day of destruction following a period of apostasy. You would expect the Old Testament to be full of judgement, and the New Testament to be full of hope, but the canonical order here ends with impending judgement on the people of God at Jesus' Coming.

This fact stands as a solemn reminder and warning to the Church not to be complacent, believing herself to be safe on the Day of the Lord. The great danger is not persecution by enemies, but the falling away of believers.

The Gospel reading offers the perspective for those who look forward to his Coming: judgement does not come only at the last Day, but begins with Jesus' presence already. 'As I hear, I judge', Jesus says (5:30). The basis of the judgement? Jesus' word dwelling in us (5:38). The daily test of faith is how we live by the word that he has spoken to us (cf 15:3). This is not, however, a new legalism, or a faith based on a task. The word which has been spoken to us is, 'Love one another as I have loved you' (15:12).

We now live 'between the times'. We look for the Coming of our Lord Jesus; yet, he is already here. Our anticipation at this time of year is that of those who looked for the redemption of Israel in the First Century; but we know he is here. As we await him, we live out our faith, longing for his return, but seeking for his will to be done now, in our own time.

Dwight D Swanson,
Senior Lecturer in Biblical Studies

Endure patiently, hope expectantly!

Zechariah 1:7-17; Revelation 3:7-13; Matthew 24:15-31

All three of our passages for today ring with the Advent call to faithful endurance and expectant hope. Zechariah's was the voice of God's mercy, comfort and undying covenant love to the remnant of repatriated exiles from Babylon, who after 20 years had only managed to rebuild the altar of sacrifice and reset the temple foundations (see Haggai 1-3). Jerusalem was in ruins and deserted. Opposition from prosperous nation-neighbours and the struggle to survive left them despondent, disillusioned, and without motivation to continue the mission of restoration.

Into this, the promise of God's presence, and overflowing prosperity for Jerusalem shattered their darkness and despair. Even so, his covenant love must be met with their covenant response (Zech 1:3, 16-17). In return, the Lord Almighty will dwell with them. Jerusalem will be a city of peace. They will look forward with expectant hope, to the coming of their righteous king, gentle and riding on a donkey, bringing salvation, proclaiming peace to the nations (chs 8-9).

The scene in Matthew 24 is quite different. The Jews are a subject people again. The second temple has been extended by Herod the Great. When the disciples praise the magnificence of the structure, Jesus predicts a time coming (realised in AD 70) when this temple, in all its glory, will be razed to the ground. The followers of Christ must watch for the approach of the forces of desolation and destruction. Faithful obedience to God's alarm signal will be their only hope of deliverance, which will come only after the period of distress and darkness!

Revelation takes us to a faithful congregation in Philadephia whose limited strength and resources are severely stretched in the face of severe persecution, yet they have kept his word and honoured his name. In recognition, Christ holds open before them the 'door of opportunity' for which he alone holds the key.

Their message is a call to continue to endure patiently with the promise that he is coming soon and will deliver them from the fierce trial to come (v 10). This Advent call to faithful endurance and expectant hope is as valid for us today as ever it was!

Clive Burrows,
Pastor, Bolton,
Acting Field Coordinator, CIS, Eurasia Region

— 36 —

It's about how we live here and now

Zechariah 2:1-13; Revelation 3:14-22; Matthew 24:32-44

As a young Christian I was scared by the 'left behind' stories that were being promoted at that time. These were based largely on the verses from Matthew 24 about there being two people in the field and one would be taken and one left behind. What I had failed to grasp from these verses was the much deeper and richer lesson that Jesus was trying to give: that what is important is what we are doing with our lives and how we are living here and now. At Advent we reflect with joy and hope on the great truths that Christ will come, Christ comes and Christ came. We live in the 'in-between times'; the time between Christ's first and second comings. No one knows when that day will come – not even Christ – but how we live now is hugely important. What are we doing to reflect kingdom values in our lives and in the life of the Church?

A favourite image of mine as a young Christian was the picture of Christ from Revelation 3, knocking on the door of our heart to gain entry. But again is there not a deeper theme here? The Laodiceans are accused of being 'lukewarm'. They think they are doing fine but in reality they are anything but fine. Christ requires faithful living; those who are fully committed to him. He disciplines those he loves because he desires us, his people, to lead holy lives. The discipline comes in the context of Christ coming to have fellowship with us, to eat with us. One day when Christ does come again that fellowship with him will be complete. We will have a place with Christ and in a wonderful sense the prophecy that Zechariah gave to the returning exiles to Jerusalem will be fully realised: 'Sing and rejoice, O daughter Zion! For lo, I will come and dwell in your midst, says the Lord' (2:10).

This Advent time, as we think about Christ's return in glory, may that hope spur us on to live faithful, disciplined lives until he comes.

Alison Yarwood,
Registrar

Worship and praise of the Holy God

Zechariah 3:1-10; Revelation 4:1-8; Matthew 24:45-51

In the fourth vision of Zechariah, Satan lobs an accusation against the high priest Joshua, probably to symbolise the uncleanness of the priesthood and the people of whom Joshua was representative. God has saved his people from captivity but the restored nation had to be cleansed if it were to be established. God's people are to walk in his ways and keep his commands (Zech 3:7). These are unchanging conditions for our acceptance and for God's continued blessings upon our ministries. Joshua, the leader of the community, is a type of the Messiah whose first coming we celebrate at Christmas. Zechariah's vision ends with a peek at the coming Messianic age when Christ returns to establish a kingdom that is characterized by peace, justice, and security.

John saw a little more than Zechariah did. He was ushered into heaven 'in the Spirit' where he saw the events that would take place when Christ returns. The twenty-four elders, who, probably, are representatives of the redeemed of the Old Testament and New Testament, join together in the worship of the God of glory. Together with the four living creatures, they offer continual praise to God. They do not cease night and day from singing the praise of God (Rev 4:8). Their song begins with the threefold, 'holy, holy, holy' (Isa 6:2, 3), thus signifying that the holiness of God must be central in acts of worship and praise. God is holy in all aspects—in his majesty and moral excellence.

Given such a great privilege awaiting us, how then should we live? Christ's return demands faithfulness by his followers. The call to faithfulness is accentuated in Matthew's parable of the faithful servant. Hence he warns us to be faithful and wise, not to grow lax or presumptuous as we wait in the event that he does not come when we expect him to (Mt 24:48). We must be ready, not in terms of sitting and quietly waiting, or indulging in selfish exploitation, but being involved in the service to others. We must also remember that God will be the determining judge of our actions (v 51).

Ayo Adewuya,
Professor of New Testament,
Pentecostal Theological Seminary,
Cleveland, USA

Not despising the day of small things

Zechariah 4:1-14; Revelation 4:9-5:5; Matthew 25:1-13

God has a way of taking the seemingly insignificant and making it into something momentous. Throughout the Bible we see countless examples of insignificant people, objects and places that become significant to the story of God. Isn't it the elderly Abraham and Sarah that produce the heir through whom all nations will be blessed? Isn't it the unlikely shepherd crook of Moses that becomes the 'staff of God' through which God performs His miracles to lead His people to freedom? Isn't it in the Judean wilderness that the voice heralding God's imminent arrival is heard?

In Zechariah 4 we encounter Zerubbabel, a man charged to rebuild the temple in Jerusalem. The first temple was built in glory, celebrated with fanfare and was forever associated with the great kings, David and Solomon. But now returning from exile in Babylon, with no royalty, no flourishing nation, no fanfare, and no grand opening, the task of rebuilding the temple is left to a Persian appointee. The occasion was deemed inconsequential and peripheral. What should have been a momentous day of 'great things' was in fact deemed a day of 'small things'… but not to God. 'Who despises the day of small things? People will rejoice when they see the plumb line in the hand of Zerubbabel' (Zech 4:10). In the story of God the second temple became a crucial centre of worship, work and witness and features prominently in the pivotal purposes of God despite its humble and small origins.

Centuries later, born under Roman occupation, in an obscure inn, placed in a cattle trough by his teenage parents is Jesus Christ, seemingly insignificant… but in the purposes of God the most significant of all. God has a way of breaking into human history in unlikely ways, at unlikely times through unlikely people. And so let us learn not to despise the day of small things… small acts of random kindness, small faithful ministries and churches, small gifts of time and generosity, for in God's ongoing story the small may yet be revealed as the most significant of all.

Trevor Hutton,
Director, Momentum,
Lecturer in Church Development and Evangelism,
NTC

Practising what we are professing

Zechariah 7:8 – 8:8; Rev 5:6-14; Matthew 25:14-30

One of America's greatest athletes, Marion Jones, said in her 2004 autobiography, 'I have never taken drugs and I never will take them'. In 2007 she was exposed in court as a drug cheat. There is something deeply disappointing about people who don't practice what they profess.

I now mix with more 'unchurched' people than 'churched'. Their main objection to Christianity is that we are like Marion Jones; we don't practice what we profess. That's a gross generalisation and not the whole story but we must admit that it is part of the story. Maybe, it's always been so. God complains through Zechariah (Zech 8:9-11) that his people were not practising what they were professing. The people of Israel weren't living out what they said they believed about Yahweh.

Jesus' main point in his parable in Matthew 25 seems to be that those who join his revolution can't be passive. His disciples have a responsibility to put their faith into action and grasp the opportunities that confront them. Both passages remind us that authentic faith in the God we encounter in Scripture is never just about intellectual belief; it always expresses itself in concrete ways through our behaviour.

I know of no clearer reminder of this than the 'Lamb, looking as if it had been slain, standing in the centre of the throne' who confronts us in Revelation 5. Jesus is presented as the messianic king because he has been faithful to his calling as the Lamb of God. What Jesus professed, he practised. He believed he was the Suffering Servant and embraced the way of the Cross it entailed. In Advent we remember we are waiting for Christ to return but these passages remind us that we are not to wait passively but actively by putting into practice what we profess. Today let's look for those God-given opportunities to express our belief in concrete ways through our behaviour. Let's follow the example of Jesus Christ rather than Marion Jones. Revelation's lesson for us is that Christ's way results in a glory that will never tarnish.

James Petticrew,
'Mosaic', Edinburgh Church Plant,
Mission Officer, Scottish Episcopal Church

Seeing Jesus in the eyes of others

Zechariah 8:9-17; Revelation 6:1-17; Matthew 25:31-46

We'd rather not think about final judgement and grim predictions about the fate of others. It doesn't sit well with our notions of a loving God, certainly not at Christmas.

We can easily figure out who Jesus is referring to when he mentions sheep and goats. Some people choose to extend kindness while some get caught up in their own agendas. We see it every day. Sometimes, we're even guilty of it. But, given the harsh imagery surrounding this rather homely reminder of kindness, is there more going on here? I tend to think there is, and uncovering it is almost like peeling an onion – there are layers of meaning.

We begin by seeing Jesus in others. It seems fairly obvious that as Christ followers we have an obligation to those in need. After all, that's what Jesus did. Yet, it's not just the caring that matters to Jesus – it's the reason why. It is easy for us to see the other person as an embodied need; to pity them, rather than to come alongside them. When we adopt a stance of superiority we can easily make the other feel inferior. That's not the Jesus way.

— 45 —

While Jesus could be referring to biological siblings, he really has something else in mind. In Matthew 12:50 he said, 'Whoever does the will of my Father in heaven is my brother and sister and mother'. In other words, how we take care of other Christ followers matters. It's about seeing Jesus in our family – our church family.

There is another layer to peel off here – to recognise the weak and broken person within all of us – to see Jesus in myself and my needs and frailties. It is easier to see that in another person than to see it in myself. Can we learn to discover more of Jesus in those moments when we feel weakest?

Hebrews 12:2 reminds us, 'Let us fix our eyes on Jesus, the author and perfecter of our faith'. Do you see Jesus when you look into the eyes of those who need you? And do they see Jesus when they glance back at you?

James Paton,
Associate Lead Pastor, Foothills Alliance Church,
Calgary, Canada

He came to heal us from the fall

Genesis 3:8-15; Revelation 12:1-10; John 3:16-21

Following the Sunday morning service which I had led, a visitor approached me. Why, he asked, had we repeated the statement, 'Lord, have mercy', so often in the worship service? The person had never encountered this type of worship. The actual statement in the service was, 'Lord, have mercy; Christ have mercy; Lord, have mercy'. What seemed obvious to me appeared unusual and, perhaps, unnecessary to him.

In the Scriptures for today we begin to understand the meaning of asking Christ to give us his mercy and love. The Genesis reading is the follow-up to the story of the temptation in which Adam and Eve fell from the mercy and grace of God. It was the fellowship with God that preserved their lives in the Garden. But now everything had changed. Now, instead of independently standing up to God, they hid themselves from God's presence. Along with the hiding came the blaming; each blamed someone else. The narrative reveals the seriousness of the problem; the lesson is clear. Sin has a devastating effect on our lives. Life now enters into a prolonged death experience and there is no way out!

But the story does not end in hiding, blaming, and, ultimately, in despair. The story moves to reveal another, continuous event, 'God so loved the world'. The problem of the serious devastation of sin has not been left to our floundering, feeble efforts. From the beginning God loved creation and humanity. Even if humanity had severely 'messed up', God offers a deeper sense of hope and confidence. God not only loved the world, God sent his only Son.

The anticipation of the Advent season is one of hope and celebration. The Son has entered into our human condition to restore and heal our broken lives. To paraphrase the idea offered by the second century theologian, Irenaeus, he went through every stage of our development in order to heal us at every stage of our development.

So we can say, 'Lord, have mercy; Christ have mercy; Lord, have mercy'. In his mercy and love he entered into our lives to restore and heal us from the devastation of the Fall.

David L Rainey,
Senior Lecturer in Theology

Anyone for golf?

Zephaniah 3:14-20; Titus 1:1-16; Luke 1:1-25

He had served his denomination with integrity for forty years as a pastor. Every year he concluded his pastor's report with a joke. Some were better than others. All reflected his philosophy on life and ministry. He stood before his peers and delivered his final report with this joke: an Irishman was walking with his friend. In the distance he saw some men hit a small white ball with a stick. 'What are they doing?' he asked. 'Playing golf', was the reply. His friend tried to describe the intricacies of the game, an almost impossible task. They decided to follow the golfers. One man hit his tee shot into some trees. 'He'll never get it out of there', the Irishman said. He watched in amazement as the golfer hit his ball out of the trees, and he followed it as it ran into a deep bunker. 'He'll never get it out of there', repeated the Irishman. Again, in utter disbelief, the Irishman watched the golfer play a chip shot onto the green and he watched as the ball rolled into the hole. The Irishman shouted, 'Well there's one thing for sure, he'll never hit it out of there!'

It was not one of his better jokes. His captive audience laughed in the right place to humour the old preacher. Then he made his application of the story. 'There have been days in my ministry when I have been in the trees and I thought, "I'll never get out of here". Other days I was bunkered and again I thought, "I'll never get out." Today I play my final hole. My ball goes into the 18th hole but my ministry is not over. Today I will take my ball out of the hole and will place it on to the first tee and will watch a young man drive it straight down the centre of the fairway. If he will let me, I want to be his caddy.'

For the remaining four years of his life he walked with that young pastor. He assisted him in getting out of some tight situations and advised him on how to avoid some awkward traps. The young man did not always hit the ball down the centre of the fairway, but he always had his caddy to help him in the rough.

Paul saw something worthwhile in a young man called Titus. He referred to him as 'My true son in our common faith' (Titus 1:4), and he poured his life into him. He helped Titus to be a good worker for Jesus Christ. Who are you helping to become a better player in the kingdom?

Philip McAlister,
Field Coordinator, North Europe, Eurasia Region

A child brings deliverance

1 Samuel 2:1b-10; Titus 2:1-10; Luke 1:26-38

I bring good tidings of a Saviour's birth
To you and all the nations upon earth:
This day hath God fulfilled His promised word,
This day is born a Saviour, Christ the Lord.

Hannah was grateful to her God for the child Samuel, whom he gave to her in response to her cry. In her song of personal praise and thanksgiving she delights in the Lord who has brought deliverance to her. But more than this, through the lens of her private joy, she has caught a glimpse of the God who hears the cries of those who are suffering and acts powerfully on their behalf. She anticipates a day when God will defeat wrong, bringing about the salvation of his people through a kingly reign. This expectation, partly realised in King David, finds its ultimate fulfilment in the birth of Jesus Christ.

And so centuries later the angel Gabriel came to Mary to announce the birth of that one who would be given the everlasting throne promised to the Messiah descended from David (2 Sam 7:13, 16). The angel makes it clear that the holy one to be born to Mary is the one through whom God will accomplish his redemptive purposes. His name will be Yeshua, 'The Lord is Salvation'. Mary is overwhelmed by this incomprehensible message so she humbly accepts that what God has declared will certainly happen. She too rejoices in God her Saviour.

Titus recalls the momentous birth of the long-awaited Messiah-king, speaking of it in terms of the grace of God bursting in upon humankind. Grace comes freely from the hand of God; salvation is a gift. Through the sacrifice of our Saviour Jesus Christ we are redeemed. And we too rejoice. Yet the response to grace and the effect of grace operative in our lives should lead to holier living. So Titus challenges all believers to live godly lives so that the miracle of transformation God has effected in Christ will be attractive to all. Thus the kingly reign glimpsed by Hannah and foretold by the angel will extend to the ends of the earth.

Mary Wood,
Bible Teacher, Sharpe Memorial Church, Glasgow,
Member, Board of Governors, NTC

I will be to him a father

2 Samuel 7:1-17; Titus 2:11-3:8a; Luke 1:39-56

'I will be to him a father and he shall be to me a son'. God's promise to David obviously refers in the first place to Solomon. But the words of this 'covenant' which God made with David (see 2 Sam 23:5) may now be seen to have a fuller fulfilment. Mary rejoices in God her Saviour in this psalm or hymn which we call the 'Magnificat' (after its first word in the Latin version). From her 'great David's greater son' is to be born, and she rejoices that he at last will right the world's wrongs. He will be the true king to rule for ever, to bring down the oppressors and exalt the deprived and exploited.

So the words, 'I will be to him a father', gain a new meaning. Her son Jesus will indeed be 'the Son of God'. But we need to be careful here. It is not that God becomes the father of this One because of his human birth of Mary. That would be a pagan, indeed a blasphemous, idea! The God of Israel is not Zeus. It is rather that this One, now to undergo human birth, has been the unique Son of God from all eternity. That is to say that he, like the Father, is fully and truly and eternally God, just as the Father is.

That is clear in the passage from Titus. Mary called God her 'Saviour' in her song, but in the letter to Titus, 'our great God and Saviour' is identified as 'Jesus Christ'. It was God himself who came in the person of his Son and took human flesh from Mary in order to be our Saviour. Our Saviour Jesus is indeed God Incarnate. Charles Wesley sang: 'Veiled in flesh the Godhead see'.

How then are we to respond? Like Mary, we should respond in heart-felt thanksgiving and praise. Whatever our cares and worries this Christmas – health problems, money (lack of it!), loneliness, children who are far from God, or whatever it may be – the great king is coming to be our Saviour, and, at the last, he will right every wrong and make all things well. God is with us!

T A Noble,
Senior Research Fellow, NTC,
Professor of Theology,
Nazarene Theological Seminary, Kansas City, USA

We're waiting...

Isaiah 59:15b-21; Philippians 2:5-11; Matthew 1:18-25

...and it's nearly time! All the anticipation, the contemplation of judgement, all the preparation, all the longing, and we're on the brink of Christmas – our time of Advent contemplation, of looking deeply at ourselves, our characters, our lives, our world is being met by the celebration of Christ-amongst-us – God-with-us.

We are at the point of retelling our story – where all the looking forward comes to its climax, and we gather together again to recite the good news of great joy – so we tell it over and again, to our children, and our children's children. We tell the story that unites believers all around the world: Where God humbles God-self, and shares our humanity, and enters into our midst; where salvation is revealed as being for all people – all men, all women, all the insiders, all the outsiders, all are welcomed into the kingdom. Where God's promise of making us right with God – of our being part of God's family, God's own children, heirs, sons and daughters, is being made real – here, now, amongst us. And so the challenge to us is to align ourselves with this movement from God. At Christmas we are to be revealed as people who have the same attitude as Christ Jesus. We are to be people who see that God loves us, and because of God-with-us we respond; the whole of our beings declaring that Jesus is Lord, to the glory of God the Father.

What does this mean that Jesus is Lord? What does his Lordship look like around this time of year? Perhaps it means that we examine our lives and depose other lords – perhaps it means we depose the lord of greed, or consumption... Perhaps we challenge the lord of busy-ness, or the lord of hard-heartedness... Perhaps it means we depose the lord of family feuds and long, cold silences... Perhaps it means that we depose the lord of gloom and practice joy-bringing-passionate-Jesus-following into the new year...

On this day, perhaps it means that we pray in thanksgiving, declare with our whole hearts, and celebrate with the whole of our being that God-With-Us, Jesus, who saves us from our sins, is amongst us.

Deirdre Brower Latz,
Lecturer in Pastoral and Social Theology, NTC,
Pastor, Longsight, Manchester

'But when the time had fully come...'

2 Samuel 7:18-29; Galatians 3:23-4:7; Luke 1:57-66

Jesus came into a world of unique opportunities and challenges. The Roman Empire was dominant. Roads, well paved and engineered, made travel safer and more rapid than at any time until the 19th century. While displacing Greece as the Mediterranean power, the Greek language became widespread as the language of culture and commerce. There was tolerance of religion. Judaism was accorded preferential treatment, being called the *religio licita*, and the new Christians were able to capitalise on their association with it. The Jews were scattered throughout the Roman Empire and wherever they went they carried the knowledge and worship of one true God and the hope of a coming Messiah. Christians, scattered following the persecution of Stephen, began to share the Good News 'as far as Phoenicia, Cyprus and Antioch, telling the message only to the Jews' (Acts 11:19).

This becomes a great missiological moment: 'Some of them, however, men from Cyprus and Cyrene, went to Antioch and began to speak to the Greeks also, telling them the good news about the Lord Jesus'. So, what began as a Jewish movement controversially crossed major cultural and religious barriers to pagan Gentiles. This was a risky business and it caused all kinds of discussion in the Jerusalem church! But the gospel had made a significant cross-cultural leap and, as they say, the rest is history.

History is still being written. The geographical centres of Christianity have changed over the centuries. When the Edinburgh 1910 missions conference was called, the 1200 delegates came 'from every point of the compass…', and people marvelled at the cultural and geographical translatability of the gospel. As the Edinburgh 2010 conference is planned, no doubt it will reflect on the new global centres of the faith in what were once traditional mission areas.

As we celebrate this Christmas, a challenge that faces us is to make the translation of the gospel where we live, in our 'known world'. This is where the gospel needs to be culturally embodied and theologically translated. As we look for ways into people's lives (Acts 17:16ff) we are spurred on by the reality that in the fullness of God's time, Christ will come in his Second Advent. *Gloria in excelsis Deo!*

David McCulloch,
Principal

Lightning Source UK Ltd.
Milton Keynes UK
16 November 2009

146302UK00001B/1/P